Every Day I'm Awesome!

A Guide To Positive Thinking For Kids

Written By: Jessica Sykes

To my youngest son Anthony,
For inspiring me to have a positive outlook on life.
You're Mr. Awesome!

-JS

ISBN: 978-0-578-41755-4

Printed in the United States of America 10 9 8 7 6 5 4 3 2 1

Every day I'm awesome because every day, I say I am. Remind yourself how amazing you are daily and you will become just that.

(Repeat) Every day I am awesome!

Every day I'm awesome because I will shine bright like the stars. I will stand out from the crowd and hold my head high through everything.

(Repeat) Every day I am awesome!

Every day I'm awesome because I respect myself as well as others. Treat others how you would like to be treated.

(Repeat) Every day I am awesome!

Every day I'm awesome because even when I am afraid, I will try to be brave. Being brave is doing something even though it makes you nervous.

(Repeat) Every day I am awesome!

Every day I'm awesome because I love helping my family and friends. Always lend a helping hand when you can and others will help you in return.

(Repeat) Every day I am awesome!

Every day I'm awesome because I turn learning into fun. Learning can be a great experience just use your imagination.

(Repeat) Every day I am awesome!

Every day I'm awesome because I love to make myself and others happy. Choose to make yourself and someone else smile today.

(Repeat) Every day I am awesome!

Every day I'm awesome because I will try my best and push myself harder then yesterday. Keep going no matter how hard it may seem. Hard work always pays off. Never give up.

(Repeat) Every day I am awesome!

Every day I'm awesome because I will be kind to everyone.
Showing kindness will surely warm your heart.

(Repeat) Every day I am awesome!

Every day I'm awesome because I think and act with a positive attitude. Whenever a bad thought enters your mind, replace it immediately with a good thought or a happy memory.

(Repeat) Every day I am awesome!

Every day I'm awesome because I will keep my mind and body healthy. Staying active and eating healthy, will help you feel good about yourself.

Every day I am awesome!

(Note to self)
Write all the things that make you awesome and what you will do
to become better.

Manufactured by Amazon.ca
Bolton, ON

13514693R00017